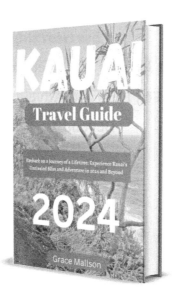

# KAUAI

## Travel Guide

Embark on a Journey of a Lifetime: Experience Kauai's
Untivaled Bliss and Adventure in 2024 and Beyond

# 2024

Grace Mallson

# Table of Contents

## Introduction

I arrived on the alluring island of Kauai on a bright, sunny morning. My heart glowed with enthusiasm as a curious traveler eager to see the treasures that this tropical paradise had to offer. I had no idea that I was about to have the most remarkable event of my life.

I arrived at the Napali Coast trailhead after a leisurely drive along the picturesque shoreline. It was a stunning site that tempted me to set off on an incredible trip, with lush emerald cliffs towering above. I started the challenging yet thrilling journey with a bag, camera, and a wanderlust.

The trail wound its way through deep jungles that were teeming with exotic birds and softly whispering leaves. I discovered a hidden waterfall that was cascading down a moss-covered ravine as I continued on my journey. I felt as though I had found my own personal oasis as the cold mist caressed my skin, and I couldn't resist having a cooling swim in the crystal-clear lake below.

As I continued on my quest, I came across a breathtaking vista point that offered a panoramic view of the craggy cliffs of the Napali Coast and the azure expanse of the Pacific Ocean. It was a humble experience that made me appreciate the incredible beauty that nature has to offer.

As the day came to an end, I traveled to the Wailua River, which is renowned for its verdant valleys and calm waters. I decided to go on a kayak expedition and paddled around the riverbanks while taking in the peace and quiet of the area. I suddenly became aware of a covert entrance leading to a sinister cave. I chose to continue my exploration after becoming overly curious.

As I entered the cave, the ethereal glow coming from the bioluminescent algae on the walls astounded me. It had the impression of being like entering a mythical realm where time had stopped. I was in awe of the beauty that nature could provide as I watched the cave appear to reveal more of its secrets with each step.

The island still held more delights in store for us, and the day was far from ended. I traveled to Polihale Beach, known for its magnificent sunsets and golden dunes, as the sun started to set. I felt at peace as the sun dipped below the horizon, illuminating the sky with orange and pink hues, and I knew I had found my own little piece of heaven.

When I thought back on my trip that evening, I saw that Kauai had given me more than just a great experience—it had also allowed me to feel deeply connected to the beauties of nature. The unspoiled beauty of the island had made an everlasting impression on me, and I was aware that this trip was merely the start of a lifetime love affair with Kauai's undiscovered treasure.

I found myself mesmerized by Kauai, the Garden Island of Hawaii, as the golden sun fell beyond the horizon. It lured me to go on an unforgettable voyage with its beautiful landscapes, azure waters, and friendly aloha atmosphere. I had traveled there eager to experience the captivating culture and breathtaking natural beauty of the island.

Tip 1: Adopt the Aloha Spirit.
The inhabitants of Kauai exude warmth and friendliness. Respect others, embrace the aloha

spirit, and pick up a few Hawaiian words to communicate with the locals.

Tip 2: Honor nature

From majestic cliffs to peaceful beaches, Kauai is home to stunning landscapes. Practice Leave No Trace ethics and safeguard delicate ecosystems to show respect for the environment.

Tip #3: Invest in some rain gear.

Weather might change quickly, so be prepared. Bring rain gear because showers can be powerful but short-lived. Don't let the rain bring you down; it frequently produces stunning rainbows.

(4) Rent a vehicle

Rent a car to experience all of the island's varied sceneries. This enables you to go off the beaten track and find undiscovered jewels.

Fifth recommendation: Visit the Na Pali Coast.

To see the NaPali Coast's untamed splendor, go on a boat cruise or a trek. Your jaw will drop at its majestic waterfalls and towering rocks.

Try local cuisine, the sixth tip

Enjoy Kauai's delectable cuisine, which includes fresh seafood, tropical fruits, and classic Hawaiian fare like poi and kalua pork.

Attending a luau can help you fully experience Hawaiian culture. Discover traditional customs, take in hula performances, and eat a regal feast.

## Tip 8: Honor Sacred Places

Numerous heiau (temples) and cemeteries are among Kauai's sacred locations. Respect these sacred spaces by not interfering with them.

## Tip 9: Be careful around water

The ocean is not always predictable. Swim only in specified areas where lifeguards are present, and be aware of rip currents.

Tip 10: Look for waterfalls.

Discover the magnificent waterfalls of Kauai, including Wailua and Opaekaa Falls. When viewing these natural treasures, keep safety precautions in mind.

I thought back on the priceless experiences I created in Kauai as my trip came to an end. This Garden Island has completely won my heart, from the welcoming smiles of the residents to the stunning scenery. I left with a renewed sense of awe for the beauties of nature and a profound admiration for the aloha attitude that permeates this enchanted location. Kauai had shown me that excitement and serenity could coexist peacefully, making it a place unlike any other.

# Visa Requirements

I once set off on an exhilarating journey to the beautiful island of Kauai. I was excited to discover the region's natural treasures and fully acquaint myself with the colorful Hawaiian culture because I am a curious and enthusiastic traveler. I had to traverse the complex world of visa regulations, though, before I could enter this paradise.

I was relieved to learn that Kauai accepted visitors from a variety of nations and that obtaining a visa was pretty simple. I just required a passport that was valid and had at least six months left on it because I was a citizen of a nation that didn't require a visa. I was eager to get on the plane as soon as I had all my paperwork in order.

I felt at ease when I arrived thanks to the immigration agents' friendly grins. They said "Aloha" to me and gave me a waiver of my need for a visa for 90 days in order to go. As a result, I had plenty of time to explore the island's beautiful scenery, which ranged from the majestic Na Pali Coast to the tranquil Waimea Canyon.

I was enthralled by the dynamic culture the entire way. I participated in customary luaus, picked up the hula dance, and ate delectable Hawaiian cuisine. I developed enduring friendships and was made to feel at home by the locals.

I experienced a mixed-up sense of satisfaction as my time in Kauai came to an end. I had taken in the wonders of the island and its rich history. I left Kauai with treasured memories and the desire to one day return, as well as a heart full of appreciation.

In addition to Kauai's natural beauty and cultural appeal, getting a visa was an easy process, making the trip truly memorable. It helped me make priceless memories that I would always cherish by teaching me the importance of being well-prepared and following local laws.

Additional information on Kauai visa requirements
for visitors is provided below:

**Absence of Visa**: Since Kauai is a part of Hawaii, tourists from a wide range of nations can visit without a visa. You can stay in Kauai for up to 90 days without a visa if you are a citizen of a nation that does not require them. The United States, Canada, the United Kingdom, Australia, Japan, and the majority of the European Union nations are among the nations that do not require visas for travel.

**Continuity of passport:** If you want to enter Kauai without a visa, your passport needs to be valid for at least six months after your intended departure date. Before departing, it is crucial to confirm that your passport still satisfies this criteria by checking its expiration date.

Visas for nations that are not exempt: You must apply for a tourist visa at the closest American embassy or consulate in your home country if you are a citizen of a nation that is not on the list of nations free from visa requirements. You will apply for a B-2 Tourist Visa, which is the sort of visa.

**How to Apply for a B-2 Tourist Visa:** To apply for a B-2 Tourist Visa, you must provide the following items: a fully-completed visa application form, a current passport, a recent photograph, proof of your travel plans, evidence that you have enough money to cover your stay in Kauai, and possibly additional supporting documents as specified by the embassy or consulate.

You must pay a non-refundable visa application fee in order to be considered for a B-2 tourist visa. It is important to verify with the embassy or consulate for the most recent charge because it may change.

Processing Times for Visas: Processing times for visa applications can change based on the workload at the embassy or consulate. It is a good idea to apply for the visa well in advance of the dates you intend to go.

Kauai is a part of the U.S. Visa Waiver Program (VWP), which enables nationals of particular nations to visit the United States, including Hawaii, for brief stays without getting a visa. Travelers covered by the VWP must, however, get a valid

ESTA (Electronic System for Travel Authorization) before boarding a trip to the United States.

To ensure a simple and enjoyable vacation to Kauai, don't forget to confirm the individual visa requirements for your nationality and plan your trip appropriately.

## Top 10 Places you can't Afford to miss in the City

The "Garden Isle," generally known as Kauai, is a tourist haven with breathtaking scenery, immaculate beaches, and a lively culture. The following are the top 10 attractions in Kauai City you simply must see:

**Na Pali Coast:** Take a boat, a helicopter, or go hiking to explore the stunning cliffs and green valleys of the Na Pali Coast. You'll be in awe of the stunning scenery.

**Waimea Canyon:** Often referred to as the "Grand Canyon of the Pacific," Waimea Canyon features breath-taking panoramic vistas and hiking routes that wind through colorful red and green landscapes.

**Hanalei Bay:** Surrounded by lush mountains, this lovely bay is ideal for swimming, surfing, or just lounging on the golden sand.
Witness the cascading grandeur of Wailua Falls, a well-liked location for touring and taking breathtaking pictures.

**Poipu Beach Park:** Unwind on Poipu's warm shores and take advantage of the chance to see humpback whales or Hawaiian green sea turtles in the winter.
Limahuli Garden and Preserve: At this botanical garden, you can take in the splendor of indigenous Hawaiian plants and discover more about the rich cultural heritage of the island.

**Kalalau Trail:** For experienced hikers, set out on the difficult but rewarding Kalalau Trail, a 22-mile journey through the pristine nature of the Na Pali Coast.

Explore the lovely village of Hanapepe, which is renowned for its vibrant art galleries, old structures, and Friday night art stroll.

Visit the Kilauea Lighthouse, a historic site and nature sanctuary, where you might be able to observe seabirds, dolphins, or perhaps whales from the cliffside overlook.

**Spouting Horn:** At Spouting Horn, take in the stunning natural display of water flowing through lava tubes to create a beautiful water spout.

The City of Kauai ensures that every visitor has an exceptional experience thanks to its stunning natural beauty and dynamic culture. Don't pass up the chance to discover this magical island and make lifelong memories.

## Hotels with a low cost and their prices

During a mesmerizing summer, I set off on an exciting journey to the mythical island of Kauai, which is renowned for its lush scenery and captivating beauty. I was determined to experience this paradise on a shoestring budget as a wise tourist. I started looking for inexpensive motels that wouldn't sacrifice comfort because I was curious and wanted to maximize my trip.

I discovered the "Seaside Serenity Inn," a wonderful tiny hotel tucked away near the island's magnificent beaches, after days of thorough study and evaluating various possibilities. To my surprise, the accommodation prices were fairly inexpensive, making it the ideal starting point for my island adventures.

I was welcomed at the inn with warm smiles by the welcoming personnel, and the welcoming atmosphere put me at ease right away. Even though the accommodation was basic, it had an unmistakable charm and a balcony that provided stunning views of the ocean as dusk fell. My luck was just unbelievable!

I had a free breakfast every morning that was packed with local delicacies, setting the mood for my day of exploring. I set out to explore the island's various beauties with the help of my reliable map and guidebook.

Mystical Napali Coast, flowing Wailua Falls, and all of Kauai's other natural treasures left me in amazement at every step. I enjoyed the sensation of the soft sand beneath my feet on the lovely beaches as well as hiking through lush jungles and swimming in hidden waterfalls.

As the days passed, I noticed that I was assimilating into the lively island society. The islanders were very friendly and invited me to take part in their customary luaus and storytelling events. My visit was greatly boosted by the lively culture and gracious hosts.

After a day of exploration, I would come back to the Seaside Serenity Inn's comfort in the evenings. I spent evenings there under the starlit sky, mystified by the sound of the waves smashing on the coast, its peaceful atmosphere a shelter for my weary soul.

My stay on the island was coming to an end as the days grew into weeks. Bidding farewell to Kauai and the new friends I had made there was difficult.

My heart will always be filled with the memories of the island's beauty, the friendliness of its residents, and the right balance between my budget and life-changing experiences.

So, as I flew back to my home country, I brought with me more than just a collection of photos and trinkets; I also brought with me a spirit of adventure and thankfulness for the enchanted voyage I had in Kauai. This story showed me that one can find enchantment everywhere in the world, even on a tight budget, and that the experiences that stick with you the most are the ones that are braided with threads of curiosity, exploration, and real connections with other people.

## Budget Friendly Hotels

Located in the center of Kauai's South Shore, the "Tropical Hideaway Resort" provides comfortable lodging at a reasonable cost. This beautiful hotel offers a tranquil setting and convenient access to surrounding attractions including Poipu Beach and Spouting Horn, with rates starting at roughly $100 to $150 per night.

The "Island Breeze Inn" is a great value and is tucked away in the sleepy hamlet of Kapaa on

Kauai's East Coast. It is a wonderful option for tourists wishing to discover the island's picturesque treasures, like the Sleeping Giant Trail and Wailua River, because prices normally range from $80 to $120 per night.

"Beachcomber Hotel": The "Beachcomber Hotel" in Wailua might be the best option if you want to be close to the coast without breaking the bank. You can have a relaxing vacation close to the stunning Wailua Beach and Opaekaa Falls for prices that range from about $120 to $180 per night.

"Kauai Palms Hotel": Located in Lihue, the "Kauai Palms Hotel" provides simple lodging at a reasonable cost. The typical nightly rate is between $90 and $130, giving it an affordable choice for those who wish to check out surrounding sites like Kalapaki Beach and Nawiliwili Park.

"Garden Island Inn": This Lihue hotel offers a blend of retro charm and contemporary convenience at an affordable price. Visitors can enjoy a quiet stay close to attractions like the Kauai Museum and the Kukui Grove Shopping Center for prices running between $100 and $160 per night.

Please be aware that hotel rates can change depending on the season, particular offers, and other elements. Before making reservations, it's a good idea to check for updated prices and inventory. Additionally, some hotels could provide you a discount if you book directly through their websites or for longer stays. You can maximize your affordable trip to Kauai by keeping an eye out for specials and offers.

Located in Kapaa on Kauai's Coconut Coast, "Coconut Coast Villas" provide comfortable and reasonably priced lodging. Prices typically vary from $100 to $160 per night, and visitors can benefit from convenient access to the lovely Ke Ala Hele Makalae cycling route and the neighboring Kapaa Beach Park.

"Aloha Beach Resort": The "Aloha Beach Resort" in Kapaa is a fantastic choice for a cost-effective stay close to the ocean. Visitors can unwind by the beach or visit neighboring sites like the Fern Grotto and Wailua River State Park for an average price of $120 to $180 per night.

"Palm Garden Hotel": Located in Lihue, this establishment provides cozy lodging at a reasonable cost. The normal nightly rate is between $90 and $130, and travelers have easy access to well-known locations including Nawiliwili Beach Park and the Grove Farm Homestead Museum.

The beachside hotel in Kapaa known as the "Kauai Shores Hotel" offers a cost-effective choice with a lively atmosphere. Visitors can enjoy breathtaking coastal views and explore neighboring sites like Lydgate State Park and Smith's Tropical Paradise for a typical nightly rate of $130 to $200.

"Wailua Bay View Condos": "Wailua Bay View Condos" in Kapaa offer reasonably priced condo-style lodging for people looking for a home-away-from-home experience. Prices normally range from $150 to $200 per night, and visitors can benefit from the area's close vicinity to Opaekaa Falls and Wailua Beach.

As with any hotel reservation, it's wise to confirm current pricing, availability, and any exclusive deals or discounts. These extra choices should give you a wide range of inexpensive Kauai hotels, providing a memorable and cheap trip to this stunning island. Travel safely!

## 15 Best Luxury Hotels and There Cost

Some of the most opulent hotels in the world may be found on Kauai, a stunning island treasure in Hawaii that offers an unparalleled getaway to paradise. Let's explore the splendor that the top 15 luxury hotels on this idyllic island have to offer.

Suites at the luxurious St. Regis Princeville Resort, which is perched above Princeville's verdant cliffs and offers stunning views of Hanalei Bay for as little as $800 per night.

Grand Hyatt Kauai Resort & Spa: This five-star haven is tucked away among tropical plants and offers a magnificent lagoon pool for as little as $600 per night.

Koa Kea Hotel & Resort: Located along Poipu Beach's glittering shore, Koa Kea charms with its cozy atmosphere and rates that start at $500 per night.

The Ritz-Carlton, Kapalua: Although officially on the island of Maui, this luxurious getaway is deserving of notice, with rates starting at $900 per night.

Princeville Makai Golf Club & Resort: This resort is perfect for golfers as it provides access to the famed Makai Golf Course and has rates starting at $700 per night.

The Cliffs at Princeville: This tranquil getaway, encircled by lush vegetation, provides roomy condos starting at $400 per night.

Located on the south shore, the Ko'a Kea Hotel & Resort offers oceanfront views for as little as $500 per night.

Rates at this tropical haven start at $600 per night and include wide-ranging villas and an opulent spa.

Rates at the exclusive Timbers Kauai Ocean Club & apartments start at $1,200 per night and include elegant apartments and access to a private beach.

The nightly rate for Marriott's Kauai Beach Club, which has a lovely pool area and direct beach access, is $550.

A haven of peace, the Grand Resort Kauai provides suites with private lanais starting at $800 per night.

Hanalei Colony Resort is a hidden gem with rates starting at $400 per night. It is situated on the isolated north shore.

Sheraton Kauai Resort: Price per night for this kid- and family-friendly resort with a superb Poipu Beach location is $450.

The Westin Princeville Ocean Resort Villas, which provide views of the town's cliffs, have rooms starting at $600 per night.

Hanalei Bay Resort: Surrounded by thick vegetation, this hotel provides breathtaking views and rates as low as $350 a night.

Discover pure luxury and unfettered beauty at these 15 top luxury hotels on Kauai, where your tropical fantasies come true and every moment is a priceless memory to treasure forever.

## 7 Top Parks and Museums

Find out more about Kauai's captivating museums and magnificent parks, which provide visitors with an amazing experience. These seven places are a must-see if you want to fully experience the island's natural beauty and rich cultural heritage:

Visit the Kauai Museum to learn more about the history of the island, which is told through displays on early explorers, sugar plantation life, and ancient Hawaiian cultures. The history of the island is brought to life with interactive exhibits and relics.

On the north shore, you may find Limahuli Garden and Preserve, a botanical wonderland with breathtaking scenery and endemic vegetation. View expansive vistas of the Napali Coast while strolling through verdant gardens and learning about traditional Hawaiian agriculture.

Take a scenic riverboat excursion to the heart of Wailua River State Park, where you'll find the magnificent Wailua Falls and the revered Fern Grotto, where you may see authentic Hawaiian performances.

Allerton Garden: This gorgeous estate, which is a part of the National Tropical Botanical Garden, features a blend of flora and architecture and has been featured in films like "Jurassic Park." Its alluring appeal is highlighted by guided tours.

Discover the history of plantations on the island at the Grove Farm Museum. Discover the lives of early settlers as you go through historical structures including the sugar mill and plantation residences.

The awe-inspiring Waimea Canyon State Park, sometimes known as the "Grand Canyon of the Pacific," is home to spectacular vistas and a variety of hiking paths. For a spectacular sight, capture the colorful canyon walls at sunset.

Poipu Beach Park: Unwind on Poipu's sandy coastlines, a well-liked location for snorkeling and sunbathing. Your beach experience will be enhanced by the chance to see Hawaiian monk seals lazing in the sun.

The museums and parks on Kauai guarantee an enriching trip, leaving you with treasured memories of this tropical paradise. These attractions range from cultural immersion to natural wonders.

# 10 Things you can't Do in Kauai

Ten amazing things tourists can't do in Kauai should keep in mind as you set out on your tropical journey include:

**The endangered monk seals must not be touched:** Since they are legally protected, approaching them could make them feel uncomfortable.

**Don't miss the Napali Coast:** you can't drive here, but you can take an exciting boat excursion or hike the Kalalau Trail for breathtaking vistas.

**Respect holy places:** On Kauai, you can find important cultural and spiritual landmarks like Heiaus (prehistoric Hawaiian temples). Please keep your distance and treat them with respect.

Trespassing is not permitted on private property. Although the island is incredibly beautiful, some portions are held by private individuals.

**Niihau shells must not be picked up**; they can only be discovered on the nearby island of Niihau. Leave them on the shore, but ogle their beauty.

The "No Littering" regulation must be followed in order to preserve Kauai's beautiful beaches and lush surroundings.

Keep an eye on the weather because Kauai's environment can change quickly. Prior to engaging in outside activities, always check the weather.

**No smoking on trails and beaches:** Smoking is not permitted in certain areas to protect the environment.

Hula is a religious art form, thus show respect while watching performances. Be focused and keep your mouth shut when witnessing a performance.

**Avoid feeding wildlife:** despite being enticing, feeding animals can alter their behavior and be harmful to their health.

By keeping these ten things in mind, you'll not only enjoy Kauai's beauty but also develop into an eco-aware and culturally respectful visitor, leaving the island just as lovely as you found it. Aloha!

# Top 10 Insiders Tips

I was standing on the sands of Hanalei Bay in Kauai, a location I had long wished to see, when the sun slipped below the horizon, illuminating the sky with a brilliant array of colors. I had no idea that this Hawaiian paradise would provide me with more than just magnificent beauty; it would also provide me with priceless advice for other tourists.

*The following 10 insider hints will help you have an amazing trip to Kauai:*

**Embrace the spirit of aloha:** Be a part of the community by saying "Aloha" warmly to everyone. Explore the island with respect for the land, the water, and the locals.

**Follow Waterfalls Savvily:** Remember to tread lightly to protect these delicate ecosystems as you explore the hidden waterfalls nestled away in lush jungles.

Na Pali Coast sunrise: Take a boat excursion early in the morning to see the Na Pali Coast's ethereal splendor at daybreak.

Discover Hanalei Town by immersing yourself in the thriving local culture, which is home to quaint shops, art galleries, and delectable restaurants.

Hike the Kalalau Trail: For those with a spirit of adventure, set out on the demanding but worthwhile Kalalau Trail, which offers stunning views of the coastline.

**Beach Safety:** For a fun and safe beach experience, check the surf conditions before enjoying the clear waters and heed any posted cautions.

**Experience Local Delights:** Enjoy the varied cuisine of Kauai, which includes everything from fresh tropical fruits to classic Hawaiian delicacies like poke.

**Visit Waimea Canyon:** Explore the "Grand Canyon of the Pacific," where breath-taking vistas await those who venture into its depths. Snorkel in Poipu: Dive into the crystal-clear waters of Poipu Beach and encounter colorful marine life, including turtles and tropical fish.

**Stargaze in Polihale:** To cap off your Kauai adventure, spend the evening at Polihale Beach, which is renowned for its breathtaking night skies.

These insider hints can help you discover Kauai's true character and help you make priceless experiences that will last long after your trip is gone. Accept the aloha spirit, show respect for the island's natural beauties, and immerse yourself in the breathtaking beauty Kauai has to offer. Thank you for sharing this wonderful experience!

# 10 Important Items to Pack for Summer and Winter

The Garden Isle of Kauai in Hawaii is a tropical haven famed for its magnificent scenery, immaculate beaches, and dynamic culture. Packing thoughtfully is essential to a good trip, whether you intend to travel during the romantic winter months or the sun-kissed summer months. Ten things you should pack in your trip bag are listed below:

Lightweight attire brings breathable clothing, such as cotton and linen, for the humid summer heat. For enjoying the island's crystal-clear seas, don't forget your swimsuits. Layer warm sweaters for the winter and a rainproof jacket for unexpected downpours.

Sun protection: Because Kauai enjoys year-round sunshine, bring plenty of sunscreen, wide-brimmed hats, and sunglasses to protect your eyes.

Water Gear: In the summer, you'll need boogie boards, water shoes, and snorkeling equipment. For wintertime adventures, you'll need waterproof bags to keep your possessions dry while you trek and go swimming.

Insect Repellent: Carry a dependable insect repellent in the summer to stave off uninvited visitors like mosquitoes.

**Comfortable Footwear:** For summer excursions, consider sturdy sandals, while for winter exploration, consider water-resistant boots.

Binoculars and cameras: Use your binoculars to see wildlife far away while you capture the breathtaking beauty of the island.

Reusable Water Bottle: By bringing a reusable water bottle, you can stay hydrated while exploring the island and reduce the amount of plastic garbage you produce.

Travel adapters: Don't forget to pack the required adapters so that you may charge your electronics and other devices when traveling.

Medicine Cabinet: Make sure you have a first aid kit that is well-stocked with bandages, disinfectant, pain medicines, and motion sickness medication for boat journeys to be ready for any minor accidents.

Cultural Sensitivity: And last, have an open mind and a readiness to appreciate Kauai's distinctive culture. To fully immerse yourself in the culture, respect the 'aina' (land) and 'ohana' (family) values, and participate in the customs and traditions there.

By including these necessities in your luggage, you'll be ready to travel to Kauai and experience its magical winter delights or bask in the summer heat on an amazing adventure!

### My Amazing Experience

I set out on an exciting journey to Kauai, Hawaii's Garden Isle in 2022, prepared with the knowledge of what to pack for both the summer and the winter. I had no idea that the planning I had done would bring about an exceptional event that I would never forget. When I arrived in the summer, I was dressed in airy clothes, armed with sunscreen, sunglasses, and a sense of exhilaration. My water gear was put to good use as I made the decision to visit the well-known Na Pali Coast and its stunning beaches. I was in amazement of the underwater splendor when snorkeling among the vibrant marine life, and the boogie board allowed me to have a ton of fun as I floated along the calm waves. My durable footwear made it possible for me to hike the Kalalau Trail, and my camera and binoculars let me take spectacular photographs of soaring seabirds and beautiful landscapes.

I chose to extend my vacation into the winter as the days went by, which gave my voyage an unexpected twist. I dressed warmly in layers of sweaters and waterproof coats and set out on a guided tour to see the magnificent winter surf at Hanalei Bay. I was able to fully enjoy the magical island experience because my waterproof bags kept my items dry and safe while on boat tours.

I came across a local family participating in a traditional Hawaiian festival one fateful day as I was touring Koke'e State Park. I took part in the celebrations, dancing the hula and sampling the local cuisine with an open mind and respect for their culture. They welcomed me into their family with a warm "ohana" atmosphere, fostering precious memories that will always have a special place in my heart.

I was hydrated and environmentally conscious the entire way thanks to my reusable water bottle, which helped the island's conservation efforts. My well-stocked first-aid pack also came in handy for small accidents like mosquito stings, allowing me to concentrate on the beauties around me.

This well-thought-out trip improved my travel experience while assisting me in navigating Kauai's many weather. I was able to completely appreciate the island's beauty and culture, from the sun-kissed beaches of summer to the enchanted landscapes of winter. I have a deep gratitude for Kauai and its people because every item in my backpack contributed significantly to the creation of priceless memories. And when I said goodbye to the Garden Isle, I was confident that, thanks to the foresight of a wise traveler, I had actually experienced Kauai's beauty.

# Kauai Weather

The wonderful island of Kaui is a spot where the weather gives your trip a special touch! In the Hawaiian archipelago, the island of Kauai draws visitors from all over the world with its year-round tropical environment.

Enjoy Kauai's magnificent landscapes while basking in the sun's golden beams. With year-round average temperatures of 70 to 85 degrees Fahrenheit (21 to 29 degrees Celsius), you can enjoy a great beach day or go on exhilarating walks through verdant rainforests.

Be ready for the sporadic downpours that contribute to Kauai's lush vegetation and give it its nickname of "Garden Isle." As the island's unique flora and wildlife are nourished by these passing showers, beautiful waterfalls and bright botanical gardens are produced.

Winter delivers bigger swells to the north shores for surfers, while summer brings calmer seas for swimming and snorkeling in the clear waters.

No of the time of year, Kauai's weather offers a riveting experience, fusing the beauty of sunshine, rains, and gentle island breezes to make every visitor's trip really special. So prepare for an island vacation unlike any other by packing your bags!

# Seven-Day Itinerary

This 7-day itinerary will take you on an extraordinary journey as you discover this tropical paradise's natural splendors and cultural treasures.

**Day 1:** Get here and unwind
As soon as you land in Kauai, take in the breathtaking scenery and pristine beaches. Visit Poipu to unwind while enjoying the warm sun and azure ocean. Enjoy a traditional Hawaiian luau and a spectacular sunset at Shipwreck Beach to fully experience the rich culture of the island.

**Day 2:** Exploration of the Na Pali Coast
Join an exhilarating boat cruise around the well-known Na Pali Coast. Observe towering cliffs, tumbling waterfalls, and undiscovered sea caves. Swim and snorkel in waters that are clear and filled

with marine life. Explore the picturesque hamlet of Hanalei in the evening and eat at neighborhood restaurants to experience real Hawaiian food.

**Day 3:** An adventure in Waimea Canyon
Learn about Waimea Canyon, the "Grand Canyon of the Pacific." Hike the paths for stunning views of green valleys and red rocks. Explore the adjacent Koke'e State Park to see the local wildlife and plants.

**Day 4:** Fern Grotto and the Wailua River
To reach the alluring Fern Grotto, set out on a tranquil boat excursion along the Wailua River. Enjoy a traditional hula dance performance while submerging yourself in the gorgeous jungle.

**Day 5:** Hidden Gems of Kauai
Discover off-the-beaten-path locations like Maha'ulepu Heritage Trail, Secret Beach, and

Makauwahi Cave Reserve. Experience these hidden gems' serene beauty and seclusion.

**Day 6:** Beach hopping and a helicopter tour
Experience Kauai's unspoiled beauty from above by taking an exhilarating helicopter trip. The rest of the day can be spent beach-hopping at Tunnels Beach, Ke'e Beach, and Hanalei Bay.

**Day 7:** Surfing and Goodbye
In Hanalei Bay, take a surfing lesson from a pro or just laze around and take in the sunshine. Leave Kauai with fond memories and maybe even a glimpse of a sea turtle!
For those adventurous individuals, this 7-day trip promises an engaging experience as they travel through Kauai's various beauties.

# The top 15 outdoor activities for children

Whether you're a seasoned traveler or a first-time visitor, Kauai has a variety of fun outdoor activities for kids of all ages. Here are the top 15 outdoor activities for kids on Kauai, from exploring lush woods to splashing in clear waters:

Snorkeling at Tunnels Beach: Dive into the colorful marine life and the beautiful underwater world.
Kayaking in Hanalei Bay allows you to take in the breathtaking views as you paddle across the tranquil waters of this lovely bay.

Trek through thick jungles to reach Secret Falls, where you may take a cool plunge afterward.
Admire the "Grand Canyon of the Pacific" and its spectacular perspectives from Waimea Canyon Lookout.

Lessons in Surfing at Poipu Beach: Let your young surfers catch their first waves in Poipu's calm seas.

Ziplining Adventures: Experience an adrenaline rush as you soar through the treetops on exhilarating zipline courses.

Take a family-friendly boat excursion around the Na Pali Coast to see the towering cliffs and secret sea caves.

Visit the historic Kilauea Lighthouse to observe seabirds and catch a glimpse of humpback whales (seasonal).

Discover native plants at Limahuli Garden and Preserve while learning about Hawaiian culture.

Spend the day swimming, picnicking, and constructing sandcastles at the tranquil and welcoming Anahola Beach Park.

Riding a horse in Princeville Ranch will allow you to make lifelong memories as you gallop through the beautiful countryside.

Visit gardens, meet farm animals, and take a train trip through the plantation at Kilohana.

Take a helicopter tour to get a bird's-eye view of Kauai's breathtaking landscapes and undiscovered jewels.

Wailua River Cruise: Take a relaxing river cruise and stop at the Fern Grotto for a surreal adventure.

Kalapaki Beach: While you unwind under swaying palm trees, let your kids play in the calm waves.

In addition to the island's natural wonders, Kauai's wealth of outdoor activities guarantees that your children will have an exciting and memorable visit. Pack your luggage and get ready for a voyage full of adventures that will put both young and old at ease!

# Family Outdoor activities

With these ten intriguing outdoor activities, both families and tourists can explore the picturesque island of Kauai, a paradise in the Hawaiian archipelago.

Helicopter trip: Experience an exhilarating helicopter trip that offers stunning aerial views of Kauai's lush landscapes and jaw-dropping waterfalls.

Snorkeling at Poipu Beach: Poipu Beach is a snorkeler's paradise with pristine seas filled with beautiful coral reefs, marine life, and sea turtles.

Hiking the Na Pali Coast: Set off on a memorable hike through the rugged Na Pali Coast while discovering lush valleys, majestic cliffs, and remote beaches that can only be reached on foot.

Experience a traditional luau where you can get a taste of Hawaiian culture, savor delectable island fare, and see vivacious Polynesian dance acts.

Surfing Instruction: Learn the sport of surfing at the calm breakers of Hanalei Bay while riding the waves with your entire family.

Kayaking on the Wailua River allows you to paddle along the serene river while passing through lush trees and historic Hawaiian sites like the Fern Grotto.

ATV Adventure: Increase the thrill with an ATV trip through Kauai's difficult terrain while taking in breathtaking views of the heart of the island.

A thrilling bird's-eye perspective of the island's grandeur is provided as you speed over thick canopies, giving you an adrenaline boost.

Hanalei Bay Sunset lunch: Enjoy a leisurely beachside lunch while taking in the local cuisine and watching the sun set over Hanalei Bay.

Catamaran Cruise: Take a catamaran cruise down the coast to see playful dolphins and occasionally see whales. This is a great family excursion.

Prepare for a memorable family vacation in Kauai where you may take in the island's breathtaking natural beauty and make treasured memories that will last a lifetime. Aloha!

## 10 Best Restaurants in Town

Imagine yourself taking a leisurely stroll along Kauai's gorgeous sandy beaches, the salty ocean wind caressing your skin as the sound of breaking waves creates a tranquil symphony. The top 10 restaurants in Kauai are eager to take you on a pleasant culinary trip, and they are hidden away within this tropical paradise.

At Tidepools, where you eat in thatched-roof huts surrounded by peaceful lagoons and lit by tiki torches, the adventure starts with an unusual gastronomic experience. Only the delicious seafood meals, presented and prepared with great taste, can rival this romantic atmosphere.

Next, treat your senses at Red Salt, where a feast for the palate is created by the fusion of Hawaiian and international influences. Every meal is a work of art, from delicious Wagyu steaks to soft Ahi Poke.

Hukilau Lanai offers island-inspired food created with fresh, locally produced ingredients for people looking for a taste of Hawaii's rich cultural heritage. The distinctive Huli Huli chicken and the classic Hawaiian poke bowls are sure to make an impression.

The charming Bar Acuda in Hanalei provides a tapas-style menu that is overflowing with flavor. Enjoy their delectable paella as well as a large variety of artisanal cheeses and charcuterie.

At the St. Regis Princeville Resort, Makana Terrace provides stunning ocean views and a mouthwatering Sunday brunch with a variety of scrumptious dishes for a seaside treat.

Merriman's Fish House, a farm-to-table restaurant renowned for its sustainably sourced fish and farm-fresh vegetables, is another option on the list.

You must experience the chef's tasting menu and the magnificent ambiance.

At the historic Plantation Gardens Restaurant & Bar, which is surrounded by lush gardens, take a step back in time. You may savor regional specialties like coconut shrimp and Mahi-Mahi with a macadamia nut crust here.

Eating House 1849, where famous chef Roy Yamaguchi combines Hawaiian, Asian, and European flavors into a wonderful cuisine with excellent delicacies like Misoyaki "Butterfish" and traditional Loco Moco, is another must-visit.

Porky's Kauai offers scrumptious BBQ delicacies and fusion treats for a casual yet spectacular eating experience, ideal for fulfilling your appetites after a day of island exploration.

Finish your gastronomic journey at Kauai Grill, which is a part of the St. Regis Princeville Resort.

Enjoy world-famous chef Jean-Georges Vongerichten's inventive cuisine and inventive beverages while taking in the stunning sunset views over Hanalei Bay.

These eight eateries, located in the heart of this tropical paradise, invite you to experience a unique culinary adventure. The eating scene in Kauai offers a combination of flavors that will make a lasting impact on your taste buds and a warm memory in your heart, from elegant seaside settings to beautiful plantations. Good appetite!

# The Best Time to Visit Kauai

April to June and September to November are the best months to organize your trip to Kauai. These times of year have great weather and less tourists than during the busiest travel season. As flowers bloom and waterfalls burst with life in the spring, a beautiful canvas is painted with an explosion of hues.

In addition, traveling to Kauai in the fall offers a unique experience as the island transforms into a tranquil setting with colder temperatures, making it ideal for outdoor activities like hiking and exploring the island's verdant pathways.

Wintertime on Kauai's renowned North Shore offers plenty of possibilities for avid surfers and adventure seekers to catch some spectacular waves from December to March. Powerful surf is a sight to behold and draws experienced surfers from all around the world.

The summer months of July and August, on the other hand, offer milder temperatures, making them ideal for relaxing on sun-kissed beaches, participating in water activities, or simply taking in Kauai's breathtaking coastline.

If you prefer a more laid-back and leisurely vacation, however, you should visit during these months.

Anytime you travel to Kauai, you'll discover hidden treasures and cultural treats. Take on the Aloha spirit and become familiar with the traditions and customs of the area. Don't miss the opportunity to visit the magnificent Waimea Canyon, often known as the "Grand Canyon of the Pacific," or go on a boat excursion down the Napali Coast to see towering cliffs and gushing waterfalls; both are absolutely unforgettable experiences.

The best time to visit Kauai will depend on your choices and interests because it is a paradise just waiting to be found. No matter what kind of vacation you're looking for—adventure, leisure, or cultural exploration—Kauai will unquestionably leave you with priceless memories and a desire to visit its alluring shores again. Pack your bags, embrace aloha, and set out on an extraordinary vacation to experience the best of Kauai.

# Kauai's Busiest Season

As the "Garden Isle" of Hawaii, Kauai is a paradise on Earth with beautiful scenery and a vibrant cultural heritage. While the island is a dreamy place all year round, there are some periods when its attractiveness deepens, drawing throngs of visitors eager to discover its delights. Let's explore the vibrant splendor of Kauai at its busiest!

Bright Summers: From June through August, Kauai sparkles like a gem in the Pacific. Visitors are encouraged to embark on unique excursions by the nice climate, lengthy daylight hours, and clear skies. While nature lovers explore the breathtaking Na Pali Coast, studded with green cliffs and gushing waterfalls, surfers converge on the North Shore to ride the famed waves of Hanalei Bay.

Festive Winter Escapes: December to February sees a spike in tourists looking for a pleasant getaway from the chilly weather. Holiday festivities, hula shows, and energetic luaus bring Kauai's festive spirit to life. Accept the magical ambiance of Waimea Canyon, fittingly known as the "Grand Canyon of the Pacific," where colorful sunsets paint the skies.

Flora in Full Bloom: From March to May, Kauai's flora awakens, creating a mesmerizing wonderland. While the Hanapepe Art Night entices tourists with its artistic allure, the Allerton and McBryde Gardens create a symphony of brilliant hues and scents.
The lush vistas of Kauai become even more colorful during the rainy season (November to March). Explore secret waterfalls in the jungle or zip through the treetops by braving the weather and engaging in adventurous activities.

Extraordinary Whale Watching: Watch the beautiful humpback whales travel to the warm Hawaiian seas from January to March. Visit these gentle giants up close by taking a boat trip.

Whatever the time of year, a trip to Kauai will be one to remember thanks to the island's distinctive fusion of natural splendors and island culture. If you welcome the busiest moments with open arms, you'll find a compelling island that enchants you and leaves you craving more!

# Conclusion

In conclusion, Kauai is an unmatched jewel in the Hawaiian archipelago and a paradise that has captured the hearts of numerous tourists looking for an experience they will never forget. Visitors are in awe of the seductive tapestry of natural beauty that is created by its verdant landscapes, flowing waterfalls, and golden beaches. This island beckons visitors with an alluring mix of excitement, tranquility, and cultural diversity, asking them to embrace the "aloha" mood and immerse themselves in a world unlike any other.

Travelers are enthusiastically greeted by Kauai's inhabitants, who kindly share their customs, histories, and rich legacy from the time they set foot on the island. The island's appeal comes from more than just its beautiful landscapes; it also comes from the sincere relationships made with its residents, who kindly provide insights into the island's history and customs.

Visitors come across the beauty of nature everywhere they go as they travel the rocky terrains and winding pathways of Kauai. A visual symphony of breathtaking beauty is produced when the emerald green of the Na Pali Coastline, the grandeur of Waimea Canyon, and the ethereal glow of the Wailua Falls combine. Exploring these sights increases one's sense of adventure and appreciation for nature in general.

With a variety of sports like snorkeling, surfing, and paddleboarding to partake in, Kauai's attractiveness extends to thrill-seekers and water aficionados as well. A portal to an undersea realm filled with rich marine life, the island's crystal-clear waters give visitors an unforgettably magical chance to engage with the wonders of the ocean.

Tourists are mesmerized by Kauai's stunning sunsets as the sun descends below the horizon, painting the sky in shades of pink and orange. When this happens, the island's mystique truly comes to life, leaving people feeling incredibly grateful for having the chance to see such genuine beauty.

In the end, Kauai transcends its role as a travel destination and transforms into a treasured memory for those who had the good fortune to explore its shores. Travelers learn about the aloha spirit and the significant effects of embracing it here, in addition to the beauty of the natural world. As the sun says goodbye for the day, visitors depart the island vowing to return someday in order to experience Kauai's loving embrace once more. They also have a newfound respect for the beauty of life. The sounds of their laughter and the imprints they leave behind, which call others to follow in their footsteps and find their own slice of paradise, serve as a tribute to Kauai's enduring attractiveness until that time.

Made in the USA
Las Vegas, NV
16 November 2023

80932204R00046